KRISHNA MOHAN AVANCHA

The What of Marketing

Contents

1 The Introduction   1

2 The core marketing fundamentals   3

3 What does the question 'What' signify?   9

4 How you end up hurting through Mar-
   keting while aiming to...   14

5 The 'What' that start-ups need to focus
   on in Marketing and...   17

6 The 'What' that mid-size companies
   need to focus on in...   45

7 How the right marketing strategy can
   remove your other...   54

8 The 'What' that big companies need to
   focus on in Marketing...   63

9 How to include Gamification as part of
   your Marketing Mix   76

10 Gamification as part of your Content
    Marketing Strategy   82

11 How to make your marketing go Viral?   89

1

The Introduction

This book is dedicated to all my fellow marketing colleagues who are currently struggling to find the right steps for marketing their products or services in the pandemic era. Remember guys/girls the fact which should always drive marketing is simply the need or the requirement of the customer. If you understand your target audience and can appeal to their need to buy or consume your product or service you will never have to market ever again. Also, remember actual marketing does not feel like marketing at all. True marketing is so far from promotions and ads that it just so happens to appeal to the most even without having to tell anything to anyone. If you can appeal to the need of the customer then automatically without the need to go through sales cycles you can achieve your 5-year targets within a month's time. The effort has to be made to understand and mark the customer needs rather than just trying to reach to everyone to tell them about your product or service.

What is wrong with marketing these days?

Let me try to explain this with an example of an orchestra:

Imagine you are in the audience of an orchestra where the conductor of the band is unable to sync the various musicians to one tune. The problem with marketing is the same as some instruments tend to make more sound than the others and need to be handled correctly, an experienced musician knows the loudness of his instrument and plays it at the instruction of the conductor with the right set of instructions without which the whole music created is just noise now imagine being part of 100 such orchestras at the same time. Your audience is also exposed to such noise on a daily basis. Now imagine that while this form of noise is being played on there is a band whose conductor is able to play a piece of very soothing music, regardless of all the noise around and without the need of microphones or loudspeakers still all the people will be drawn to this as this conductor is able to bring his team together to sync something melodious. This is the effect that one can get with the right conductor at the top of the musical specialists.

2

The core marketing fundamentals

Much the same as any structure is based on a durable establishment, advertising relies upon a solid, ground-up methodology, or all else may disintegrate.

Advertising achievement isn't gotten from a solitary beating colleague, a profoundly productive innovation joining, or one fruitful mission. All things being equal, a solid promoting center layers in progress from numerous missions, points of view, colleagues, and partners.

Establishing a solid framework is more difficult than one might expect, and it expects groups to make a stride back and genuinely gut check where their victories stand. This is particularly evident on the off chance that you've been working at a "nothing new" attitude without causing a commotion.

Reconsidering your showcasing establishment may prompt conceding past disappointments or conflicting assessments.

However, there are advantages to making a stride back, including having a fair and open discussion about your business, anticipating potential, and adjusting desires. Sounds positive, isn't that so?

Keep perusing underneath as we reveal the five basics that assemble an establishment for a solid advertising center.

1. Business

It might seem like promoting and business establishments are discrete monsters, yet that is essentially not the situation. On the off chance that your business centers (lifecycle stage, normal deals cycle, income objectives) are not lined up with your showcasing centers (yearly spending plan, number of advertising workers, promoting objectives), you can anticipate skewed desires.

The arrangement of business and promoting objectives brings about a more sensible objective setting, characterized spending plans (inner and organization expenses), and timetables.

While surveying your business centers to layer into advertising methodologies, ask these inquiries:

What's our upper hand? How might we market it?

How's our client assistance? In the event that we acquire a business, will client assistance rates endure?

What's our capacity to bear hazards? Is it true that we are up for an inventive showcasing effort that has obscure outcomes, or do we need to stay with what we know?

What's our general organization vision? In what capacity can be promoting get us there?

Answer these inquiries and evaluate your advertising potential when you pursue Marketing Score. Showcasing Score is a free evaluation apparatus and promoting insight motor that mechanizes the cycle. You give knowledge into 10 center regions, and it conveys examination and suggestions that drive results.

2. Ability

How great can your advertising be without a determined, execution hungry group at the center? As per MarTech Advisor, "The greatest test in building a [marketing] group is that there are unlimited prospects and no 'right' approach to do it ."

As you construct a more grounded showcasing center, consider these ability related inquiries:

What are the jobs and duties of my current group? Are there holes in their abilities?

How might we improve effectiveness and profitability across the group?

Are there zones we can improve our way of life as a way to pull in top ability?

Remember that promoting groups vary by headcount, positions, work history, and abilities. There's no ideal proportion that characterizes the number of colleagues you ought to have or what jobs equivalent outcomes. What drives the accomplishment of one group may not decipher across all showcasing offices, particularly as you look across businesses, verticals, and objectives.

3. Innovation

Goodness, innovation… all it's advertisers' closest companion, correct? Between promoting mechanization and man-made brainpower, innovation diminishes manual assignments, speeds upcycles, and gives us better information.

However, holes in your innovation stack, obsolete arrangements, or undeveloped colleagues can cause more damage than anything else. That is the reason it's advantageous to survey your present advances, zeroing in on inquiries like:

Do we unmistakably comprehend the highlights, usefulness, and estimation of our current tech?

Are the current advancements being completely used by our advertising group?

Are redundancies inside our answers prompting failures?

What are we never helping to up with developments in advertising innovation items and administrations?

4. Procedure

A solid showcasing center goes inseparably with a thoroughly examined and explored advertising methodology. A review by CoSchedule revealed that advertisers that have a recorded technique beat those that don't by an astounding 538%.

A very much reported technique is tied in with executing with an aim, adjusts exercises to objectives, and should pull in key experiences about your business, target personas, territories of development and that's just the beginning. Think about the accompanying inquiries:

What makes our organization extraordinary, and what's our offer?

What are our present objective business sectors, and by what means will those advance in the following 1 - 3 years?

Are there any achievements (item refreshes, industry exercises) in the following 6 - a year that would be exceptionally applicable to promoting procedure?

Need assistance constructing your procedure without any preparation? Realize why a Marketing Growth Hackathon goes before solid system creation.

5. Execution

Toward the day's end, your showcasing center should be execution driven. On the off chance that it's not, how might you demonstrate MROI on any showcasing effort, procedure, or strategy you dispatched?

Ordinarily, understanding your advertising execution begins by characterizing KPIs and objectives for each. Start with questions like:

- Have we characterized month to month, quarterly, and yearly objective qualities for needing KPIs?
- Would we be able to ascertain the ROI of showcasing generally and at a mission level?
- How are KPIs at present being followed and observed?
- Do we have a normalized scorecard and revealing cycle?

3

What does the question 'What' signify?

Showcasing is the way toward showing purchasers why they ought to pick your item or administration over those of your rivals, and is a type of enticing correspondence. It is comprised of each cycle associated with moving an item or administration from your business to the customer. Showcasing incorporates making the item or administration idea, recognizing who is probably going to buy it, advancing it, and moving it through the proper selling channels. There are three basic roles of showcasing:

Catching the consideration of your objective market

Convincing a buyer to buy your item

Giving the client a particular, generally safe activity that is anything but difficult to take

On the off chance that the target of your business is to sell more items or administrations, at that point promoting is the thing that causes you to accomplish that objective. Anything that you use to speak with your clients in a manner that convinces them to purchase your items or administrations is promoting, including publicizing, online media, coupons, deals, and even how items are shown.

Four Stages of Marketing

Organizations should experience numerous phases of showcasing to guarantee their items or administrations are prepared for selling.

Ideation: Marketing begins when you build up a thought for an item or administration. Prior to dispatching an item or administrations, you should choose what you are selling, the number of choices that are accessible, and how it will be bundled and introduced to customers.

Examination and testing: Before you can take your thought public, you ought to perform advertising exploration and testing. Advertising offices normally test new item ideas with center gatherings and overviews to measure purchaser interest, refine item thoughts, and figure out what cost to set. Investigating your rivals can help you set an ideal cost and produce thoughts for situating your image in a current market.

Promoting: The data you assemble in your examination will assist you with characterizing your showcasing technique and make a publicizing effort. Missions can incorporate various types of media, occasions, direct promoting, paid associations, advertising, and that's only the tip of the iceberg. Prior to starting a publicizing effort, set solid benchmarks that you can use to quantify how powerful that promoting effort is.

Selling: Determine where and how you intend to offer to clients. Purchaser item organizations, for instance, offer to wholesalers who at that point offer to retailers. In the modern market, the purchasing cycle is longer and includes more chiefs. You may sell locally, broadly, or even universally, and a few organizations just sell their items or administrations on the web. Your appropriation and deal channels sway who purchases your items, when they get them, and how they get them.

The Four Ps Model of Marketing

The four phases of promoting can likewise be planned onto another mainstream showcasing model known as the Four Ps of advertising. The four Ps in this model is item, value, advancement, and spot.

Item: The systems you have set up to guarantee that your items are prepared for selling. Your item (or administration) should fill a hole on the lookout, address the issues of clients, and stand apart from the opposition.

Value: The expense of procurement, including both the retail cost just as less quantifiable compromises that a client should be happy to make when they buy your items.

Advancement: The data you give buyers through focused promoting to create interest in your items. Advancements normally have one of two purposes: create leads or start real buys.

Spot: Refers to how and where items are sold. All appropriation choices are essential for your general promoting measure.

Sorts of Advertising

There are numerous sorts of publicizing that you can use to advance your business, show clients your items, and create deals. Print, radio, and TV crusades are kinds of publicizing, as are regular postal mail, email, and web showcasing. On the off chance that you have a site, it should be advanced for a search to help clients discover it through web indexes like Google, Yahoo!, and Bing. Bulletins, public statements, and articles are likewise types of showcasing used to catch leads and create deals. A few organizations likewise use reference promoting, where fulfilled clients allude others (regularly for a prize) to build a business.

The ascent of web-based media stages has expanded the significance of web-based media promoting, incorporating associating with clients via online media by convincing them to follow your business, banding together with web-based media influencers through item situation or paid sponsorships, and paying for publicizing on stages like Facebook or Instagram. The kinds of publicizing that you pick will rely upon your spending plan, sort of business, and the inclinations of your optimal clients.

The Marketing Lifecycle

Publicizing, or advancement is just a single part of your

promoting plan. The showcasing cycle starts with the thought for your item and proceeds until that item is in the possession of a customer who got it. Even after a client has made a buy, your showcasing shouldn't end—a bit of your publicizing should be focused on current clients to guarantee they remain clients and increment unwaveringness.

4

How you end up hurting through Marketing while aiming to find better answers or leads.

As an entrepreneur or promoting planner, developing your image is a need. Staying aware of advancements in the public eye is significant to get purchaser criticism and keep a decent standing. Then again, there could be variables that are disrupting your business without knowing it. Workers may not understand the harm that is being done before it's past the point of no return. The following are some key brand botches that could influence your image's drawn-out future.

What I mean here is extending the brand's situating excessively far, as certain organizations need to get to a wide scope of likely clients. This system normally comes from the dread of imparting to a particular section of the market and thus restricting potential deal openings. Nonetheless, by projecting a net to everybody conceivable and not building up an unmistakable brand character, your business can crash and burn from the opposition and become effectively failed to remember. Dodge this misstep by setting aside an effort to recognize what makes your image special and what target crowd will wholeheartedly acknowledge its main goal!

We as a whole love to admire our effective rivalry to get a handle on a superior viewpoint on the thing our image is bringing to the game. However, continually evaluating our benefits and misfortunes towards others can really hurt efficiency and innovativeness to settle on more imaginative choices. By what other methods would notable brands like Nike, Adidas, and Gymshark separate themselves and win a market in the event that they all took a similar course of brand situating? Make sure to keep a sound assessment of what your image is explicitly progressing admirably, and what it can develop without precisely replicating the strategies of different central participants in the game.

Utilizing a blend of web-based media stages can be a proficient method to fabricate a solid brand, yet there is a fair compromise to arriving at likely clients. For instance, a counseling firm ought to incorporate keeping a reliable and connecting with LinkedIn and Facebook account, however, does it need a refreshed Pinterest or Snapchat account? Make a point to do a little research and find where your intended interest group can be reached and stick predominantly with those stages. In the event that you need some help, contact advertising research substances like Hubspot or Salesforce to pick up understanding and pinpoint your key segment.

Sharing substance or an excessive number of statuses on an

everyday premise can be over the top excess for a brand, particularly if the brand needs to pay attention to themselves. In the long run, your supporters will become weary of flooding their online media accounts too regularly. Things being what they are, how frequently would it be a good idea for you to post to Facebook, Twitter, and so on? It will shift depending on your after size, the organization's own calculations, and how dynamic your adherents are. An extraordinary dependable guideline is to post once every day on Instagram, up to three times each day on Facebook, and a couple of times each week on LinkedIn. A large portion of your image's web-based media should be comprised of high caliber and fascinating substance. We need to attract individuals, not push them away.

5

The 'What' that start-ups need to focus on in Marketing and how to achieve the same

For beginning phase new companies, input is regularly more significant than clients. The quicker you can resolve client complaints, and improve the item to coordinate market interest, the more probable you are to prevail upon the since quite a while ago run.

In this section we will take a gander at seven basic parts of establishing the frameworks for a forceful promoting methodology.

Finding Your Core Channel

Development hacking – incorporating promoting into your item

Transformation rate advancement

Utilizing Facebook promotions to comprehend your crowd

Client input circles

The dispersion of development and focusing on early adopters

Adjusting your informing

Separation

#1 Finding Your Core Channel

At the point when you're beginning, the main target is to discover one center advertising channel that, when zeroed in on, turns into your development switch.

Unexpectedly, this expects you to deliberately explore different avenues regarding numerous channels almost immediately to dispose of low-performing channels and discover one that has all the characteristics of a triumphant center channel.

Contingent upon what stage your startup is at, you'll likely need some sort of framework for organizing your showcasing thoughts, catching bits of knowledge and aligning your promoting procedure.

To do this you could utilize a stage like TrueNorth, or simply a bookkeeping page like the one in the article connected to beneath.

At the point when you're done with this post, I'd suggest

perusing this article on the S.T.A.R showcasing framework, which really expounds on the most proficient method to dispense your promoting spending plan from the beginning to recognize your center channel and has a free bookkeeping page format for dealing with your advertising cycle.

I can't help contradicting Fred Wilson's statement, yet I can't question that the best startup showcasing procedures are those that install advertising into their item.

Dropbox, Hotmail, Eventbrite, Mailbox, and Snapchat broadly obtained a large number of clients with basically no cash spent on promoting. Their mystery? Incorporating virality into their item.

A startup's capacity to become famous online relies upon two factors: time, and the 'viral coefficient' for example the quantity of new clients every client produces.

The following is a diagram to delineate startup development at various rates dependent on changing viral coefficients. Envision that the Y-pivot speaks to your number of client information exchanges, and the X-hub speaks to time.

In the event that your viral coefficient is 1.0 (every client creates one new client), you will accomplish direct development, expecting you hold your clients. On the off chance that you have a viral coefficient above 1.1, you will accomplish remarkable development as shown by the entirety of the lines over the lower green line.

How would you implant promoting into your item?

Each startup is special, so I won't examine strategic techniques in incredible detail. There are two wide systems I'd suggest, however: The first is to fabricate an item worth suggesting. On the off chance that each and every client suggests two new clients, you have dramatic development.

The least demanding strategy for estimating a client's probability to suggest your startup is by utilizing the Net Promote Score, a basic test where you ask clients "on a size of 1-10, how probably are you to prescribe our item to a companion?" If the total score is above 9.0, you will probably accomplish remarkable development.

The subsequent methodology is to adjust your 'development hack' with the channel(s) that your optimal clients use to find out about your item. Brian Halligan from Hubspot put it best when he stated:

With regards to development hacking, it's awful if your development hack produces huge presentation for your image on Facebook – when 99% of your best-fit clients coming from perusing B2B whitepapers. In the event that that were the situation, a superior methodology is produce client created content that could be utilized to scale delivering top notch whitepapers.

It very well might be less provocative than the development hacking contextual analyses covered by TechCrunch, yet it'll work.

#3 Conversion Rate Optimization: Increase your information exchanges with split-test tests

Change rate improvement (CRO) is the science behind agreement why your guests are not 'changing over' into clients, and afterward improving your informing or incentive to build this pace of transformations. In spite of prevalent thinking, it doesn't begin with running A/B tests; it begins with understanding your guests and their protests.

Step by step instructions to recognize client protests:

The quickest method to comprehend why potential clients are not changing over is to ask them. The following are a few instruments and procedures that I'd suggest.

Introduce Intercom – an extraordinary device that permits you to talk continuously with site guests.

Request that guests round out a review utilizing Survey Monkey. Ordinarily, you'll need to boost this with some sort of giveaway.

Request criticism in a gathering your clients partake on.

Commission some client tests from UserTesting.com.

Welcome somebody you know (a client) to lunch/Skype.

Following this, ideally you will have a smart thought of what is keeping your guests from changing over. Presently it's an ideal opportunity to make changes to your point of arrival to counter these complaints.

The primary thing I'd suggest is zeroing in on the zones with the most influence. Zero in on your features, call to activities, and lead catch structures. Use devices like Leadformly, which will give you a high-changing over structure without going through months split testing various varieties.

The accompanying model by WiderFunnel is likewise an awesome beginning stage for seeing how to improve the probability of a transformation. At whatever point I am given a CRO venture, I like to consider how we could improve each point. For instance, would we be able to diminish the route to limit interruptions? Would we be able to expand the direness by having a commencement clock or a "Solitary X left" close to our call-to-activities? In 2012, I figured out how to fourfold a site's transformation rate from 2.5% to 10% utilizing these techniques.

When you have your mockups planned, I prescribe utilizing Visual Website Optimizer to test them against your current point of arrival. VWO has an extraordinary UI, making it exceptionally simple to rapidly test varieties of your site without expecting to make backend coding changes.

Change rate streamlining isn't something you do once. You ought to endeavor to continually change and improve your greeting pages to make steady enhancements.

Simultaneously, consistently recall the model underneath. Gradual changes will consistently hit a cutoff. There's frequently undeniably greater open door in being intense and testing something altogether different.

#4 Facebook Advertising: Finding your ideal crowd utilizing division

The vast majority consider Facebook Ads a securing channel for driving information exchanges. Actually it's likewise extraordinary compared to other client research apparatuses we have accessible to us.

Allow me to clarify. There is no restriction to how finely you can section a Facebook advert. On the off chance that you needed, you could run an indistinguishable adverts to 500 diverse segment and psychographic crowd sections. Utilizing change following, you can see which socioeconomics and psychographics then have the most elevated transformation rate on your administration.

Here are a couple of models. I work with numerous music new businesses, and I've discovered consistently that guitarists are normally bound to join to a music administration than a drummer or a bassist. For one of our customers, FanDistro, we found that 23 year old Canadians are around 3x bound to change over than long term olds. We realize that artists in New Zealand are bound to change over than Australians.

Facebook Ads are, as I would see it, the most ideal approach to rapidly and moderately check who your crowd are, and what your expense per-securing is for various segment gatherings.

#5 Installing a Customer Feedback Loop

It merits emphasizing that the main resource for most new companies is to be determined what requirements improving, and have a light-footed framework for making those upgrades. Any individual who's perused Eric Ries' book The Lean Startup will comprehend this as the 'Emphasis Cycle'.

A basic 'give us criticism' structure isn't sufficient. The vast majority won't make a special effort to give you criticism. Use motivations, meet your clients, and study client conduct information to comprehend where individuals tumble off in your channel, and all the more critically – why?

#6 Diffusion of Innovation: Targeting Early Adopters

Numerous unpracticed advertisers tragically target the mass market too early. The explanation this once in a while works is on the grounds that most of individuals oppose change, and are not open to items/administrations that are not previously suggested by early adopters.

I took in this exercise through A/B testing. Two years prior, while running a test to see whether extra social confirmation expanded information exchange rates, I found that by just adding the quantity of preferences and clients previously joined close to the information exchange button, dramatically affected expanding the site's information exchange rate.

In the event that you need to claim the larger part piece of the overall industry, your underlying dispatch methodology and informing should interest trailblazers and early adopters. When you have various contextual analyses, tributes, and regarded trailblazers praising you enthusiastically, at that point it's an ideal opportunity to move toward the greater part. The loafers will follow.

#7 Why, What, How: Fine-Tuning Your Messaging for Conversion

In the event that you haven't read Simon Sinek's book 'Start With Why', I'd firmly suggest putting it on hand.

The substance of the book is that, in the event that you need to move somebody to make a move, you should start by clarifying why you do what you do. Not what or how.

Apple is an incredible illustration of an organization that sells "why". Macintosh shakes things up with all that they do – MacBooks, iTunes and iPads are exactly how they do that. Dell don't have a why – they simply sell sensibly great PCs. While Apple talk about pushing humankind forward and stirring things up, Dell talk about the size of their processors and RAM. Is anyone surprised why individuals line for quite a long time to get the most recent item, while Dell get not even close to the degree of promotion, regardless of their items being fundamentally the same as.

In the model beneath, Leadformly's feature is 'Catch and convert up to 300% more leads'. This doesn't enlighten guests anything regarding what or how the item functions, however it gives a convincing 'why', trailed by a subheading that clarifies what the item is and how it functions.

Does your informing impart why your startup exists? Do you know your why? If not, this is a significant advance that I would not prompt skirting.

#8 Differentiation in your promoting

Different examinations anticipate we see between 1,000 – 5,000 ads for each day relying upon where we live. How would you contend and stand apart with your promoting in quite a soaked space?

The appropriate response is by being the shepherd, not a sheep.

Our cerebrum sorts comparative snippets of data together, a cycle known as Gestalt. Along these lines, the to a greater degree something comparable we see, the less effect each extra thing has. At the point when Lady Gaga wore a dress made of meat it stood out as truly newsworthy everywhere on the World. At the point when others replicated her eccentricity, scarcely anybody talked. This example has rehashed itself a large number of times over.

This isn't about first-mover advantage; this is tied in with seeing what every other person is, and being the inverse. Apply this from the most large scale part of your technique down to the miniature, and you'll be flabbergasted at how critical this is.

Since we've covered off the establishments of informing and setting up your item for an effective promoting technique, how about we proceed onward to client securing. I've part the segment on client obtaining into three sections, paid media, procured media, and possessed media.

Part 2: Paid Media Marketing for Startups

There's a way of thinking that says new companies ought to spend as meager as conceivable on advertising. I oppose this idea. I accept that showcasing should zero in on sure ROI (rate of profitability). In the event that a paid media channel can beneficially drive qualified clients for your startup, it'd be absurd to reject it on the premise that it's paid for. Another explanation behind utilizing paid media is to build up an expense for each securing, as this will go about as a benchmark to analyze any remaining showcasing movement.

Paid media channels fall into three general classes: show, search, and subsidiary promoting. The following are a portion of the principle online channels I'd suggest investigating, alongside certain tips on each.

#8 Facebook Advertising

We've just examined Facebook Ads from an examination viewpoint, however how about we think of it as now as a channel for obtaining clients.

While it's conceivable to compose a guide of this length on Facebook Ads alone, I'll rapidly sum up a portion of my proposals dependent on a lot of Facebook Ad crusades that I've dealt with.

Use page advanced posts focusing on individuals in the news channel. These promotions have the most elevated navigate and commitment rates.

Test whatever number advert varieties as could reasonably be expected. The more irregular, more splendid, and more novel your promotion is, the better. At the point when every other person zigs, zoom.

Try not to make promotions utilizing the Facebook Ad Manager (it's terrible). Either utilize the force manager, or a devoted apparatus like Qwaya. This will make division a lot simpler.

Use change following – by introducing the transformation pixel you empower oCPM for transformation offering. This fundamentally implies that Facebook will algorithmically upgrade your financial plan for additional changes.

Utilize fine division – If you use Qwaya, you can part your advertisement crusade into tens or many individual promotions each focusing on a particular section of your crowd. This empowers you to rapidly observe which advertisement portions perform well and which don't, so you can move your spending plan to the fragments that are generally beneficial.

I've expounded on Facebook Ads in more profundity here.

#9 Google Adwords (Search)

On the off chance that your item tackles an issue that individuals look for, there's a high probability that Google AdWords will be an incredible securing channel for you. For instance, if your startup assists individuals with finding the least expensive gig tickets, you might need to offer on terms like 'modest gig ticket', 'London gig tickets', and 'Gaslight Anthem London Roundhouse tickets'.

#10 Google Adwords (Display)

Additionally to above, Google empower you to buy pennant adverts through their showcase organization. You can indicate which sites your standard advertisement shows up on, or offer to show up on sites identified with specific watchwords.

#11 Reddit Advertising

Reddit is regularly neglected as a paid promoting channel. I need to concede, the outcomes I've had in the past are incredibly fluctuated, however it's modest and consistently worth testing.

Reddit publicizing works by running promotions at your preferred highest point of any subreddit. For instance, for a music customer, we may promote in the subreddits 'WeArethe-MusicMakers', 'Music', and 'Guitar'. Each subreddit has an exceptionally unmistakable network, so it pays to engage in every one for a touch of time first prior to running advertisements.

One explicit motivation behind why I'm a devotee of Reddit Advertising is on the grounds that Reddit appears to pull in the early adopter types. It's an extraordinary spot for getting genuine input and focusing on individuals who are probably going to be responsive paying little mind to what stage your item's at.

#12 Google Remarketing

Google Remarketing goes one stage past the standard showcase publicizing referenced previously. Basically, when somebody visits your site a treat is dropped on their PC. At the point when they visit different sites, an advertisement will seem urging them to return to your site.

You can get extremely savvy with this by running distinctive remarketing promotions for various phases of your information exchange channel. For instance, in the event that they visited the information exchange page however didn't finish the structure, you could run a promotion with a motivating force to wrap joining.

Google Remarketing is for the most part exceptionally powerful as individuals you're publicizing to are qualified and right now mindful of your item. Try to get the recurrence right and not be excessively irritating!

#13 Facebook Exchange

Facebook Exchange works in a fundamentally the same as Google Remarketing, however utilizing Facebook Ads all things being equal. As such, somebody visits your site and skips. At the point when they go to Facebook they'll discover your advertisements urging them to return.

To utilize Facebook Exchange you'll have to utilize one of their accomplices. I've tried a modest bunch of them and suggest AdRoll.

#14 StumbleUpon Advertising

While the nature of guests from StumbleUpon is for the most part very low, the expense per click is astoundingly low additionally, empowering you to purchase a lot of traffic for an ease.

I've yet to see dumbfounding outcomes from StumbleUpon promotions, aside from movement related substance. StumbleUpon is exceptionally visual interpersonal organization where uplifting and animating substance appears to spread virally. In case you're an extravagance travel administrator, this is a gold mine. On the off chance that you a SAAS organization advancing an application, it very well might be somewhat trickier.

#15 Twitter Advertising

Twitter Ads can be exceptionally viable, however the explanation I haven't prescribed them sooner is because of the spending constraints. Right now, the base financial plan for a Twitter Ad crusade is £5,000/month, which is outside of most startup's spending plan. In the event that you do have such a financial plan to contribute, at that point Twitter Ads do will in general be quite successful when done right.

My recommendation is advance an astounding bit of substance instead of straightforwardly advancing your administrations.

View Twitter as a 1:many stage where, on the off chance that you run your advertisements accurately, you can dispatch your substance to a huge crowd who will acquaint your substance with a much bigger crowd.

In the event that your mission bites the dust subsequent to being elevated to the underlying crowd, start once more.

#16 Content Discovery Platforms

There are various substance revelation stages that advance your substance close by articles on significant news locales, for example, the New York Times and The Guardian.

I've tried a small bunch of these, including Outbrain, Zemanta, nRelate and Taboola. For driving backlinks and dispatching content they're an incredible asset, despite the fact that they can get very costly relying upon the nature of your substance.

#17 LinkedIn Advertising

While my own encounters with LinkedIn publicizing has not been especially sure, I am aware of a couple of new companies (especially in the monetary administrations industry) that have accomplished incredible outcomes by showing focused on promotions to individuals to their employment title and area.

As I would like to think, the issue with LinkedIn Ads is pennant visual impairment. The adverts don't stick out, and show up in a similar spot on each page, making clients become 'ignorant concerning' them.

#18 Video Pre-Roll Advertising

On the off chance that your startup has created a convincing promotion video, pre-move publicizing could be an incredible paid showcasing channel for you. Utilizing TubeMogul, you can pay for your video to show up as an advert before video content on significant video organizations, for example, 4od, and YouTube.

One fascinating 'stunt' with pre-move publicizing is that you don't pay if your advertisement is skipped inside the initial five seconds (which the vast majority do skip). The stunt, at that point, is to go down one of two courses. The main course is to get the message out about your administration inside the initial five seconds of the video trusting that individuals skirt so you can open your message to an immense number of individuals without paying excessively.

The subsequent choice is to make the initial five seconds uncertain and adequately bizarre to interest individuals to watch the remainder of the video. Here's the best model I've seen of this strategy being incorporated.

#19 Affiliate showcasing

On the off chance that your startup profits by offering a high edge item and has a decent change rate, at that point you may profit by offering a partner program through an organization, for example, Affiliate Window or ClickBank.

I wouldn't exhort plunging into partner showcasing until

you've just settled your image and discovered other advertising channels. Think of it as a greater amount of a quickening agent instead of a base fuel for your internet showcasing technique.

Part 3:Earned Media Marketing for Startups

Acquired media can be considered as any type of exposure produced by your backers (clients, fans, accomplices). As I would see it, procured media is the most important, savvy, believable, and supportable type of web based advertising. It's additionally the hardest to make and quantify.

The explanation acquired media is so compelling is on the grounds that individuals trust their companion's suggestions. Then again, our trust in for all intents and purposes any remaining types of paid and claimed media promoting is declining.

So how might you influence this move in trust to drive more deals/information exchanges?

#20 Do Something Remarkable

The mystery ingredient of the PR business is that wonderful things get commented upon. In the event that you need to acquire informal exchange and have the press, your clients, and whoever else discussing your startup, you should give them something noteworthy.

Presently, this doesn't really mean you need to assemble a full-scale mythical beast skeleton on a sea shore in Dorset, or fly jetpacks around New York City, however in the event that you need to cause a wave, you'll need to accomplish something past the standard. Maybe your startup is noteworthy in itself?

As much as I'd love to state "do X", there is no basic answer here, in light of the fact that frequently the things haven't been done before that are work the best. My best exhortation is to peruse Edward De Bono's book on Lateral Thinking (he spearheaded the word 'parallel reasoning'), get some post-it notes and impact out the same number of thoughts as you can evoke. At that point go for the possibility that is generally encouraging.

#21 Build Exceptional Resources

I battle to go seven days without referencing Moz.com's climate projection device. It's an unbelievably helpful asset for the SEO business and creates gigantic measures of exposure for Moz.

Here and there you don't have to rehash an already solved problem – you simply need to ask yourself "what might our clients discover valuable?" and fabricate something extraordinary.

#22 Meet Your Influencers

How important would it be to your startup in the event that you met Robert Scoble, Jack Dorsey, or some TechCrunch columnist? An enormous part of your achievement in PR and showcasing rotates around who you know, so it's essential to realize what influences the size and nature of your own organization.

Meeting anybody begins with being in a similar space as them, either geologically or basically. Last January I was talking at Midem, a music gathering in the South of France. While over yonder I met Robert Scoble, Mark Hoppus from Blink 182, and various intriguing individuals who've become significant contacts. I don't express this to gloat, however to mention that it was inconceivably unsurprising and all around exposed that these individuals would be at Midem on the predefined dates – all I needed to do was appear. The hardest part in gathering the individuals you need to meet is reserving the ticket and appearing.

"80% of accomplishment is appearing" – Woody Allen

#23 Search Engine Optimization (SEO)

More than 500 million individuals search in Google each day. Despite what some startup VIPs may announce, SEO isn't something you ought to disregard.

The strength of search promoting is that, in the event that you have an item that individuals are searching for, your site can show up at the ideal second – when they're looking for it.

This varies to Facebook, LinkedIn, and YouTube publicizing, where you're depending on interruption to pull individuals from what they were doing to visit your site. With Google, you're causing them find what they were searching for in any case.

Natural inquiry advertising is a wide field in itself, so I won't go into much profundity at all here. In any case, I will bestow a couple of recommendations from my experience working at a SEO organization for quite a long while, and administering many missions.

Try not to believe you're setting aside cash by recruiting a modest SEO. Rankings go the two different ways, and on the off chance that you get somebody poo, they'll cost you significantly more than you might suspect. Be set up to follow through on a fair cost for good SEO administrations.

Zero in on what's best for the clients – if all else fails, ask yourself "is this best for our clients?" – if the appropriate response is truly, there's an excellent possibility that it's likewise best for web crawlers.

Nothing is ensured. Any individual who ensures results is in all probability selling fake relief.

It requires some investment. I educate most concerning our customers not to expect any expansion in SEO traffic for in any event 3 months. Obviously, some of the time we see increments in as meager as seven days, however SEO normally sets aside a long effort to develop.

Section 4: Owned Media Marketing for Startups

Possessed media identifies with any promoting channel claimed by your startup. In the online world, this alludes to any sites and web-based media profiles that you work.

There's a lot of hybrid among claimed and procured media, and I like to consider possessed media being the 'stage' for expanding the accomplishment of your acquired missions.

Envision you made an incredible story on how your startup just broke a World Record. Without a stage to distribute the story on, you're best expectation is to convey an official statement and cross your fingers that at any rate one columnist will distribute the story.

On the off chance that you have a blog with a consistent crowd of 5,000 guests for each day, you can present your story on that crowd, and have confidence that at any rate, 35,000 individuals will have been presented to the story by one week from now. Ideally, that underlying crowd will have 'dispatched' your story making natural development.

#24 Building a Blog That Converts

Building a blog that converts is hard. Most organizations fizzle since they blog about what they need their clients to peruse, as opposed to expounding on what their clients need to peruse.

There are few organizations who get this. Cradle, for instance, are an organization that offer web-based media robotization programming. Rather than going on about their administrations, their blog contains bits of knowledge on everything from joy to composing tips. They compose what their clients need to peruse.

My recommendation when assembling a blog is this: on the

off chance that you need to make a genuinely fruitful blog, you should be eager to submit at any rate 100 extraordinary articles. After you've composed 100 articles you'll not just have a decent comprehension of what works, yet each article will be driving a smidgen of traffic, a couple of connections, and a couple information exchanges every day. From that point, the outcomes will compound.

In case you're prepared to launch your blog, look at our examination on the best web facilitating organizations to begin with.

#25 Email Marketing

Five years back, email showcasing was tied in with building your mailing rundown and sending pamphlets or autoresponder crusades out.

Those days are a distant memory. Conventional email promoting is quickly being supplanted by advertising mechanization, which is programming that enables you to trigger customized messages dependent on various guidelines. For instance, in the event that somebody pursues a free preliminary yet doesn't really utilize a specific component inside a specific measure of time, you can trigger a mechanized email welcoming them to look at it.

Promoting is at last a pursuit to send the correct message to the perfect individuals at the perfect time. Promoting computerization is probably as close as we can get to scaling this.

There are loads of incredible email advertising instruments that currently offer promoting mechanization. I for one love ActiveCampaign, which has perhaps the best interface for building advertising mechanization crusades that I've seen.

The subsequent stage is to understand what makes a decent email. This isn't just about composing interactive headlines and making excellent HTML formats, it's tied in with understanding what your crowd needs to get in their inbox. I can't disclose to you the appropriate response here, however I encourage that you consider "would I need to get this email?"

Make certain to try different things with various frequencies of messaging, days of the week, and types. Contrasting the open and navigate rates after some time is the lone sure approach to understand what works and what doesn't.

#26 Video: Leveraging the second biggest internet searcher in the World

We once in a while consider YouTube a web index, yet with more than 50,000,000 pursuits made on YouTube consistently, that is adequately what it is. Utilizing YouTube Traffic Estimator, we can see precisely the number of searches are made for various inquiries consistently.

Suppose your startup offers time the board arrangements. A snappy hunt on YouTube for recordings on profitability uncovers that numerous 3-minute recordings have more than 50,000 perspectives – some have more than 1,000,000.

#27 Content Marketing: Infographics, Videos, Case Studies, White Papers, and then some

With regards to advanced advertising, I like to consider what will work in two years time. I don't really accept that substance showcasing will be the future, yet I do feel that content-based online PR will be.

I think the cover between making outstanding substance and relationship-based PR will be what the best advanced advertisers will zero in on a couple of years from now.

I won't zero in on the relationship-based part here, as I've just canvassed that in some profundity in the segment on gathering influencers. We should rather zero in on what makes content excellent.

The initial phase in delivering outstanding substance is to characterize extraordinary. Overall, out-play out each other organization of substance by generally 198% (number of back-links and social offers). I realize that substance identifying with robbery, sovereignties, and music industry challenges is bound to be shared than content identifying with craftsman news or the live business. I know this since I measure what works widely.

You also should know, with certainty, what works in your specialty.

On creating substance of excellent quality, my general guideline is to go through over 40 hours delivering it. Anything that takes less time is effectively likely simple to duplicate. That doesn't mean you shouldn't make it, it just methods it likely won't create astounding outcomes.

Try not to begin your substance procedure with what would we be able to make? Start with what might be astonishing? You'll figure out how to make it.

For explicit tips on substance advertising, I composed a post for Moz offering 97 hints on substance promoting.

#28 Building a Presence on Twitter, Facebook, Google+, and other informal communities

Like email showcasing, informal communities give an incredible occasion to dispatch substance and drive expected clients to your administration, yet there's undeniably more to it than broadcasting your plan. Interpersonal organizations give an incredible occasion to assemble input, fabricate connections, and add validity to your administration.

While a guide via web-based media is a long ways past the extent of this guide, here are a couple of significant focuses to consider in your social methodology.

Realize why you're utilizing it

Due to the always expanding number of interpersonal organizations, and the unlimited prospects of what you can do inside online media, it's imperative to realize why you're utilizing web-based media from the beginning.

You can have various reasons. Amount isn't the issue, clearness is.

At last, retweets, likes, +1s and shares are good for nothing. Your center business objectives are what matter: client information exchanges, maintenance, income, client lifetime esteem, client fulfillment and so forth Web-based media becomes important when you interface the two together. Whenever you use Twitter to use PR openings, Facebook to build the amount of monetisable eyeballs, or Google+ to expand search rankings, that is when web-based media has a substantial worth.

Understand what works

I invest a ton of energy in media outlets understanding what substance is the most shareable. While it's acceptable to affirm these things with information, frequently it just takes a couple of long stretches of exploration to comprehend what individuals talk about in your specialty. Endless organizations distribute poo that nobody in their correct brain would have a discussion about – don't fall into that trap. Start by understanding what sparkles discussions in your specialty.

Lead with content

We deal with a good number of web-based media methodologies at Venture Harbor, and in the event that I can summarize what separates the customers who are fruitful utilizing online media from the individuals who are less along these lines, it's having a substance driven technique.

What I mean by this is that by having an ordinary stream of intriguing substance being made and shared inside your informal communities, the sum and profundity of commitment appears to normally develop and compound. It prevents you from utilizing web-based media for utilizing online media, and rather center around utilizing it as a way to a more important end.

6

The 'What' that mid-size companies need to focus on in Marketing and how to achieve the same

No organization is excessively little for a promoting procedure. Indeed, the more modest your organization, the more effective a legitimate technique could be. At least, you ought to set up a promoting system and reconsider it every year.

Here are 14 demonstrated showcasing techniques and strategies any SMB can follow.

1. Examination your market prior to sending efforts.

It's stunning the number of organizations spend promoting dollars pointlessly. This is the reason it is essential to explore your commercial center before you burn through cash on a help or mission.

There are numerous internet reviewing apparatuses that can

assist you with deciding the needs a lot of your intended interest group. Reviewing can be an advantageous venture in light of the fact that the more you spend on the study, the less you will unconsciously spend on pointless showcasing efforts.

It is likewise essential to look at your rivals on the web. This can be as straightforward as entering what a planned customer would type to discover your administration in a web crawler. While exploring contenders, you should check for any showcasing efforts they have directed.

2. Recognize target markets.

Deciding your optimal possibility's profile is a vital advance prior to creating efforts. You can utilize a more expensive help, for example, Hoovers, which produces a total rundown of the relative multitude of organizations you should target.

In any case, there are likewise other free choices, for example, ReferenceUSA. To get to this business information base you can frequently make a free record through your neighborhood library, in the event that they are supporters, and thusly, they will permit you admittance to numerous information bases. InfoUSA information bases are likewise accessible for nothing.

3. Build up an advertising spending plan.

Whenever you have explored your market, build up a year showcasing financial plan. You ought to make gold, silver, and bronze spending plans so you can without much of a stretch cut or increment spending plans consistently.

You will likewise be settling on cognizant choices NOT to direct certain missions, which is vital. For choices on setting your advertising financial plan, see our white paper "Deciding the Right Marketing Budget for Your Company."

4. Make sure your marking is understood and reliable.

There isn't anything more disappointing to a possibility than attempting to sort out what is the issue here, and discovering in the end that your item or administration isn't the one he needed. In the event that you don't comprehend the message you wish to pass on, at that point how might you anticipate that a potential client should get it?

Notwithstanding consistency of plan components, you ought to have predictable informing and situating. On the off chance that your public statements are not lined up with your site, for instance, you will incredibly confound your possibilities.

5. Plainly lucid your items or administrations.

For your customers and forthcoming customers to genuinely comprehend what you are selling, you should be clear in your introduction. This is particularly significant for administrations organizations.

Harry Beckwith, writer of Selling the Invisible, composes that administrations should be promoted uniquely in contrast to unmistakable items. In this way, it is basic to tell your customers the subtleties of what you will give so you can fulfill their inquiries. Beckwith recommends seven situating questions that should be replied.

Who right? (Your organization's authentic name)

What business would you say you are in?

For whom… what organizations/clients do you serve?

What need… what are the novel necessities of the organization you serve?

Against whom… with whom would you say you are contending?

What's extraordinary… what makes you not quite the same as the opposition?

Extraordinary advantages… what are the one of a kind advantages a customer gets from your administrations?

These seven inquiries function admirably for organizations with substantial items. By utilizing the responses to these inquiries to situate your organization, your clients and possibilities will have the option to improve comprehension of what you will give.

6. Get tributes and supports.

For likely customers to approve your contributions, it is basic to have your clients vouch for you through tributes. While tributes are typically exceptionally straightforward and simple to get, they are here and there ignored. Likewise think about video tributes, which can be considerably more successful than composed statements.

Notwithstanding filling your site with tributes, remember to request client surveys on Google, online media, or different locales pertinent to your industry.

7. Utilize verbal.

At whatever point you see a film you like or attempt another stunning café, you typically give this data to a companion or associate. Why not tailor this method to showcasing your items?

Informal promoting is certainly not another method, yet has been ignored by many advertising experts. It's tackling the voice of the client to benefit the brand, and it's recognizing that the unsatisfied client is similarly ground-breaking.

Informal Marketing Association (WOMMA) shares the five fundamental components to verbal advertising:

Teach individuals about your items as well as administrations

Recognize individuals well on the way to impart their insights

Give instruments that make it more straightforward to share data

Study how, where, and when suppositions are being shared

Tune in and react to allies, doubters, and neutrals.

8. Be very noticeable on the web.

Career expos and print promotions can be costly and are focused on inactive purchasers — individuals who are basically perusing with no aim of utilizing your administrations. For instance, a full-page notice in an exchange magazine can cost upwards of $5,000, contrasted with a compensation for each snap (PPC) crusade that can produce the equivalent or more impressions for $500–$1,000.

Likewise, online crowds have an occasion to participate in a discussion with your organization. Upgrading your online presence through SEO, PPC, and web-based media will give you a superior possibility of being found by a drew in crowd who is effectively searching for the arrangements you offer.

9. Request references.

In the event that you realize your client is fulfilled — which ideally they generally are — at that point you ought to inquire as to whether any of their companions, associates, or accomplice organizations need your administrations. Everything necessary is one basic inquiry to your customer. In spite of the fact that this sounds straightforward, numerous organizations don't do it, and lose expected business.

It is said that everybody knows in any event 250 others. Suppose you had the option to get only 20 individuals to allude only 5% of all their organization of companions, family, and partners to your business one month from now. That would result in more than 250 references to your business in only one month! This is a helpful advertising procedure on the grounds that your customers can be the best persuaders for other people, as they probably am aware your work direct.

10. Cross advance your item or administration.

Cross advancement is when at least two organizations or associations consolidate powers to publicize an item or administration, (for example, an OEM and affiliate). Each organization or association advances the other's item or administration. By collaborating with synergistic organizations, you set aside time and cash.

Key organizations will permit you to accumulate more data than you could all alone, and split expenses of more costly things, for example, promoting projects or occasion sponsorships.

11. Coordinate your showcasing.

Expansion is a key to something other than stock portfolio achievement. To successfully arrive at your intended interest group you should utilize various showcasing strategies. You should utilize various types of showcasing in equal, for example, internet promoting, advertising, advertising mechanization, and publicizing.

12. Ceaselessly impart.

Month to month e-bulletins containing enlightening articles or contextual investigations can be a powerful method to sustain leads. We suggest utilizing an advertising robotization administration with hearty highlights, investigation, and lead scoring.

13. Break down your leads.

To augment your benefits, sort out who is hitting your site. There are numerous ways you can do this, the most well known of which is Google Analytics. While Google Analytics is a free help, you may need to do some innovative structure catch, labeling, and breaking down to get the specific lead data you need.

Outsider partnership crusades are an incredible method to get your substance before an exceptionally focused on crowd, and most give definite lead reports full contact data.

14. Test consumer loyalty on a continuous premise.

It never damages to realize precisely how your customers feel and get significant input about the positives and negatives. This can be as straightforward as a call to your customers or a mysterious study on your site.

A call or email is more close to home, and your customer will realize that you esteem their assessment and business. A mysterious study, then again, permits you to really know how you led your administration or how your item functioned for your customers. This considers the correspondence of beneficial analysis, encouraging you change your items, administrations or informing. To get the best outcomes, you ought to consider leading the two sorts of consumer loyalty tests.

Making a promoting procedure for a little or medium measured business may appear to be overpowering from the start. Try not to feel forced to execute all techniques at the same time. Execute the ones that bode well for your association temporarily, and add to that establishment as you are capable.

7

How the right marketing strategy can remove your other overheads?

Quite possibly the main part of maintaining a prosperous business is showcasing your items or administrations. Without publicizing your business' strengths, you won't have the option to secure new clients.

In any case, despite the fact that promoting your business is foremost, you should be cautious that you're not overspending on advertising costs. In case you're dedicating a lot of cash to showcasing ventures that aren't procuring you generous deals, you'll be doing your business an injury in the long haul.

For some entrepreneurs, it very well may be hard to track down the harmony between putting resources into advertising endeavors and being economical so they can manage the cost of other fundamental costs, for example, lease, stock, and finance.

Try not to worry, however. It is conceivable to chop down you're showcasing spending plan without relinquishing the nature of your advertising activities. In this post, we'll furnish you with an unmistakable system so you can figure out which advertising costs you should cut from your spending plan while giving free or minimal effort thoughts to supplant them with.

We realize that making spending cuts can be testing. However, in case you're prepared to decrease your showcasing spend, start with the ventures that aren't creating deals. It very well may be frustrating to concede that a splendid thought didn't play out the way that you had foreseen, yet it is smarter to acknowledge thrashing and set aside your business' cash.

Regardless of whether this is paid social missions that aren't getting snaps or print promotions that aren't producing drives, you should free yourself of these undertakings.

Use Google Analytics or any of the stage explicit examination projects to figure out which advertising plans are low makers so they can be the first to go. You'll be in an ideal situation making the simple cut firsts and utilizing this cash for different regions of your business, for example, stock, bills, and different necessities.

You may believe that shuffling various showcasing activities immediately will be beneficial for your business, however, it really could be adverse (particularly to your wallet).

You should make room in your financial plan for quality promoting endeavors as opposed to attempting to dump cash into various normal activities. For instance, you may see that the vast majority of your leads come from internet publicizing.

For this situation, you should place more cash into this zone, rather than apportioning cash in your spending plan for thoughts that are not producing promising leads.

Put resources into showcasing endeavors that you are certain will profit your deals, and discard regions in your advertising spending that aren't strong. For this situation, less can be more!

You probably won't understand it, yet you could be burning through cash on obsolete promoting rehearses, for example, cold pitching or misleading content web-based media posts.

Prior to decreasing your promoting spending plan, set aside some effort to look into forthcoming advertising patterns. Sites like the Buffer Blog, HubSpot's Marketing Blog, and MarketingProfs will assist you with learning must-realize promoting tips that will permit you to develop your tasks. Yet, don't stop there, on the grounds that the more you read and keep up on the most recent news, the more knowledgeable you become. Here is a rundown of 16 Top Marketing Blogs and Publications You Need to Be Following, which incorporates Kissmetrics, HubSpot, Seth Godin, Moz, and Marketing Land.

You could find that you're passing up specific advancements that could improve the manner in which you market your business. As an advertiser, you need your webpage or blog, in addition to online media channels, to be the go-to asset for others in the field (or not in the field), and the best way to do that will be a stride in front of the majority.

In spite of the fact that it is essential to catch up with drives who haven't changed over into steadfast clients yet, you shouldn't burn through a lot of energy on this gathering. It is smarter to target potential clients who fit into your optimal purchaser persona, as they are significantly more prone to turn into a client.

In the event that you contact similar individuals and they persistently don't react, you're sitting around idly and cash that could be better utilized. A few organizations, in the end, discover karma with consistently reaching inert contacts, however regardless of whether you've discovered accomplishment with this previously, think about lessening your measure of touch focuses. This could assist you with transforming these leads into faithful clients, without burning up all available resources.

When lessening your showcasing financial plan, you should audit your information and guarantee that everything is genuine and forward-thinking. This could incorporate refreshing contact data or dispose of postings that are not precise or presently don't exist. This will guarantee that you don't contact people through mail who are no longer in that area or send messages to invalid locations.

Going ahead, you should focus on information association. Without putting accentuation on the exactness of your information, you could be squandering more cash than you understand unbeneficial promoting endeavors.

Make the most out of your current showcasing materials! You can do this by making an adaptable substance that you can reuse for significant stretches or for different activities.

For example, you could compose item depictions that you can add to your site, online business store, in-store flyers, and web-based media posts. You could compose a duplicate for promotion and afterward grow it into a blog entry, infographic, and explainer video.

Just repurposing substance can help you set aside cash that you'd spend to compose and plan other print or online substance.

Obviously, you'll actually need to make of kind substance for occasions and other uncommon advancements, yet for your overall valuing and choices, you ought to have clear advertising reports that you can reuse. This won't just set aside your cash in your advertising financial plan, yet it will likewise save you critical time that you can spend on different undertakings.

While there are many paid social choices, in case you're hoping to diminish your financial plan, benefit as much as possible from web-based media stages' free highlights.

Booking convincing social posts is a free, simple approach to showcase your business, particularly whenever done deliberately. You can share refreshes about your business on stages, for example, Twitter, Facebook, Linked In, and Instagram without settling on paid publicizing on these locales. Likewise, you can utilize significant hashtags to build your compass – additionally gratis!

It doesn't need to be a win big or bust methodology, by the same token. Consider restricting your supported presents to a couple of dollars daily as well as a couple of times each month, and posting natural substance on the leftover days. You'll actually have the option to target possible clients, without having to just center your endeavors (or wallet) on supported posts or promotions.

A decent method to cut your advertising spending plan, without disposing of productive showcasing thoughts, is to swear off paying external offices.

For example, maybe you work with a site improvement organization that is answerable for upgrading your site to meet SEO best practices. In the event that you or somebody on your staff knows about SEO, begin dealing with this territory autonomously. This could give an exceptional occasion to advance one of your present representatives.

You can likewise recruit a promoting or SEO assistant. Keep in mind, when you begin producing a ton of income, you can generally re-visitation of an external office or other paid assistance.

Despite the fact that this choice isn't generally conceivable (in case you're not imaginative, don't fire your visual architect!), you can quite often take on some advertising matters yourself to decrease your financial plan. There are a lot of free websites to learn SEO, advertising, and so forth

Diminishing paid promoting tasks can be testing, yet numerous entrepreneurs disregard the intensity of free exposure. You can contact nearby columnists, advertising organizations, and free public statement sites to main stories about your business or to present your public statement for quality SEO and site traffic openings.

Maybe you're holding an altruistic occasion or are divulging another item. In the event that you pitch this story to a news source, you'll get the inclusion of your business without spending a dime. This methodology isn't excessively tedious and will offer you the chance to get free business advancement.

In case you're chopping down your advertising financial plan, you need to discover free alternatives to supplant the ventures that you've been paying for, for example, informal references. You can do this by framing solid associations with your clients. This should consistently be a need, as your independent venture can't get by without faithful clients who trust in your main goal.

There are numerous straightforward ways that you can become acquainted with your clients and request their proposals, for example, making a dependability program or offering limits for references. You could likewise hold a challenge or giveaway with a cool prize on your Facebook page in which members should get the most measure of preferences on their post-accommodation to win. Make certain to declare the victor with a ton of fancy odds and ends on your page and label them, as well, to guarantee more extensive reach.

In the event that clients are energetic about your items and your brand, they'll be happy to prescribe you to their companions and become your informal image diplomats!

Notwithstanding depending on verbal references from your

esteemed clients, you ought to consider joining related systems administration gatherings, similar to the Business Network International or engage with your neighborhood office of trade.

These associations will profit your business in a horde of ways. The individuals that you meet at systems administration occasions may have the option to suggest likely clients. At the office of trade occasions, you can become acquainted with individual entrepreneurs, with whom you could work together or even co-market.

In the event that you don't as of now have a blog for your business, start one. You'll have the option to give your perusers experiences about your business' industry, your items, and other related points. In the event that you do have a blog, ensure you're posting routinely and sharing it on your social channels.

Publishing content to a blog is a mutually advantageous arrangement: you'll be showcasing your business and giving your clients free, supportive substance. In case you're simply beginning, think of one blog for each week. When you get into a predictable timetable, you can likewise compose visitor posts for related websites. This will permit you to give significant data to an all-encompassing crowd and get backlinks to your site.

Making spending cuts is rarely simple. The possibility of cutting an advertising activity and having it contrarily influence the accomplishment of your business can be scary. Ideally, with this guide, you've had the option to conceptualize ways that you can diminish your showcasing spend without harming your business' development.

Remember that your business' necessities will vary over the long haul. Your present promoting spending plan doesn't need to be perpetual; on the off chance that you dispose of activity, you can generally once again introduce it into your spending plan down the line. Whichever slices you choose to take, ensure that you're putting shrewdly in your business' showcasing!

8

The 'What' that big companies need to focus on in Marketing and how to achieve the same

Big companies might not want others to believe that they care but they too like every other company want to keep growing and adjusting. So they also want to keep their customers close to keep them satisfied & Happy which is seldom the case as they compartmentalize and attempt to reduce the overhead on one person to thus make it more complicated for every customer.

Connecting with dissemination accomplices for worldwide activities is a critical choice. Trust and ability for long haul responsibility are keys to picking the correct dissemination accomplices. Organizations likewise need to keep a tab on merchant's exercises to guarantee the usage of right organization rehearses.

Multinationals start new in deals and circulation when they enter new business sectors. Markets are broadly controlled and are overwhelmed by organizations of neighborhood mediators. Multinationals need to join forces with neighborhood merchants to profit by their ability and information on their own business sectors since they can't learn nearby strategic policies, meet administrative necessities, enlist and oversee neighborhood staff, or gain acquaintances with likely clients all alone.

Be that as it may, the connection between the global and its merchants in the new market ordinarily has a short life. Wholesalers accomplish beginning deals development by offering the worldwide's demonstrated items to their current clients. However, when extra items must be acquainted or markets new to the wholesaler need to came to, the merchant flounders.

A few wholesalers don't contribute enough and a large portion of them become content in the wake of accomplishing a specific degree of deals and pay. The wholesalers guarantee that the multinationals don't give them enough help for developing their business.

The multinationals in the end disband the merchants and control their own activities through straightforwardly possessed auxiliaries. Most multinationals have come to accept that neighborhood merchants should be impermanent accomplices to encourage their entrance in new business sectors and they ought not be depended upon to give economical development in the long haul.

A worldwide can enter a market all the more efficiently.

The accompanying rules would be useful:

1. Starting moves into new nations happen in response to proposition from possible wholesalers. Wholesalers approach organizations at exchange fairs or come straightforwardly to their workplaces. The vast majority of these merchants are serving contenders of the global and consequently have solid associations with retailers or clients. In any case organizations proceed in light of the fact that the negligible expense is low and the wholesaler bears the greater part of the danger. Yet, such occupant merchants favor business as usual and won't develop the deals of the worldwide forcefully An organization ought to methodicallly look for an accomplice in the market that it intends to enter a lot into associations with them after thorough appraisal.

2. Multinationals regularly pick merchants who know potential clients since they are now offering some contending or elective items to them. The better thought is to evaluate likely merchants as far as similarity in culture and system, the speculations they are happy to make, and the help that they would need from the organization. A global may wind up collaborating a wholesaler who doesn't have the foggiest idea about the market by any means, yet they end up being better in supporting deals development.

3. Multinationals should structure the relationship with the goal that wholesalers become advertising accomplices ready to put resources into long haul market advancement. A worldwide ought not be opposed to giving public selectiveness to a merchant. Another path is to make a concurrence with solid

motivations for proper objectives, for example, client obtaining or new item deals. Shockingly numerous organizations draw up agreements that permit them to repurchase appropriation rights following a couple of years. This gives a reasonable sign to the merchants that they are important for a momentary game plan.

4. Early responsibility of assets prompts better associations with merchants. Multinationals send specialized and deals faculty to help the merchants and give preparing to whole-salers' representatives. Some of them take minority stakes in independent conveyance organizations, which empowers co-usable promoting dependent on shared data. Just in uncommon examples have organizations removed from nations they have entered. Along these lines submitting assets early isn't as dangerous a recommendation as organizations make out

5. A merchant can be permitted to adjust a worldwide's procedure to nearby conditions however the global should practice authority about which items to offer, how to situate them and planning The worldwide needs to give promoting initiative and they ought to consistently have a portion people working with the wholesaler on location.

6. The wholesaler should be needed to famish market and monetary execution information to the global. Most merchants consider information like client ID and value levels as key wellsprings of intensity in relationship with the multinationals. However, it is significant for the global to know from where and how the incomes are being created, and if the merchant is participating in practices like value cutting, which will hurt the

worldwide over the long haul. The readiness of the wholesaler to give such data is a decent pointer of whether a fruitful relationship can be fabricated.

7. The global ought to make joins among its public wholesalers at the most punctual. The connections may appear as a provincial corporate office or a free organization, for example, a merchant board. The exchange of thoughts inside neighborhood markets can improve execution and result in more prominent consistency in the execution of the global's technique.

Some examples of how some MNC's are actually changing the way to market now:

Organizations need imaginative showcasing techniques to spread their organization message and advance their image. Gamification has become a famous system to arrive at purchasers on the web and through associated cell phones. Gaming methods, for example, rivalry, positioning records, scoring frameworks, and motivating forces—are utilized to pull in clients with the overall objective of building brand dependability, making associations, and giving clients motivation to hold getting back to the brand and buy items and administrations. The focal target of gamification as a promoting device is to help deals and increment benefit. These client arranged games have benefits that move organizations closer to arriving at their targets. They help in gathering client information, expanding commitment, boosting the organization brand and advancing recurrent business. The accompanying models show how significant partnerships are effectively utilizing gamification advertising.

M&M's Eye-Spy Pretzel

At the point when M&M dispatched a pretzel-seasoned variant of their treats, they utilized gamification and online media as a showcasing system to advance their new item. The basic and reasonable methodology included an eye-spy game that was distributed on the brand's Facebook page. They posted a realistic comprising of many, multi-shaded M&M confections and provoked their adherents and buyers to locate a little "pretzel fellow" tucked away among the confections. The game immediately became a web sensation. The Eye-Spy Pretzel game got more than 25,000 preferences, 6,000 offers, and 10,000 remarks.

My Starbucks Rewards

Starbucks applies gamification strategies through its dependability program My Starbucks Rewards as an approach to expand client commitment and guarantee rehash business. Clients who become Starbucks Rewards individuals get motivators, for example, free food and beverages, and clients get focuses or "stars" with each buy. Clients would then be able to recover these stars for explicit things or prizes. Other one of a kind prizes, for example, a free birthday drink and free tops off, become accessible as clients acquire more stars. The individuals who arrive at gold status remain to receive the best benefits. In this model, Starbucks gives motivators to gives shoppers a pride and fortifies that in the event that they are faithful to the organization, they will be compensated.

Chipotle Love Story Game

Chipotle dispatched a memory game dependent on their short film "A Love Story," in which clients should coordinate genuine fixings together while evading the utilization of added tones and flavors. Players are remunerated with a get one-get without one coupon for any food thing. Helpfully, clients can play the game and get compensates all on their cell phones. The prize urges buyers to play the game, remain drew in with the organization, and buy more, while the game itself strengthens the brand message of utilizing solid, genuine fixings rather than counterfeit tones and flavors. This is another gaming model that gives an occasion to clients to interface with the brand while carrying consideration and buzz to the organization.

Nike

The customized wellness following Nike+ and Fuelband frill take into consideration Nike to associate with their clients while gathering significant data about them. The individual information they gather is helpful for upgrading their focused on substance showcasing efforts. Nike+ Fuelband gives clients impetuses for utilizing athletic GPS beacons to go up against others while running and working out. The NikeFuel application can be connected to web-based media, which empowers clients to share and analyze achievements. Prizes and identifications are granted to the individuals who arrive at achievements and accomplish athletic achievements, which further urges purchasers to utilize their items and look for additional prizes.

Target's Wish List

Target utilized gamification advertising that was centered around kids with their Wish List application. They joined gamification with their Target Registries innovation to make an intelligent shopping list. Intended for the Christmas season, kids explore through a 3D energized game that happens in Target's Toy Factory. They simplified wanted toys to construct their vacation list of things to get and afterward send the finished rundown to Santa. The game was introduced as a pleasant route for kids to make their lists of things to get, and it's a simple path for guardians to purchase their youngsters blessings and offer blessing thoughts with different family members. The execution of the application was fruitful with the underlying dispatch creating around 75,000 downloads. Throughout the Christmas season, there were in excess of 100,000 lists of things to get comprised of 1.7 million absolute things speaking to an all out deals capability of $92.3 million.

Gamification advertising has taken off with the expanded utilization of the Internet, web-based media, and portable innovation. Games focused on an item or administration give an occasion to clients to communicate with and become acquainted with a brand. Organizations that coordinate parts of gaming into their promoting procedures will locate that straightforward and regularly reasonable games can prompt expanded benefits and more prominent web-based media portion of voice.

Some last minute tips:

We're in month 8 of the pandemic and there's one thing we know without a doubt: we miss having a good time and being near our friends and family! We miss the embraces, the chuckles, and the shoulders to incline toward. Yet, ideally at this point, we've likewise figured out how to adapt.

My method of overcoming this is messing around, either with my life partner in our loft, or for all intents and purposes with our loved ones. It's an all out need now! By what other means am I expected to disregard the infection for a second, let free, and interface with individuals over a movement?

Gamification is significant during a pandemic since it's a type of play, which gets essential for our emotional wellness when our universes have been flipped around. "Play eases pressure, permits us to communicate our actual selves, opens innovative reasoning, and gives a 'protected space' for cooperation. Joint effort, just as innovativeness, are all significant now when we require each other like never before."

Particularly during these occasions, when we're attempting to occupy ourselves from the real world, socially distance or isolate, and remain associated with our loved ones all simultaneously, perkiness is urgent. In any case, the perkiness that we urgently need to remain normal in our own lives can likewise help B2B brands remain near their possibilities and clients.

"… as senior pioneers raise computerized as an essential need, they can look to B2C organizations and enterprises for motivation." And simply like B2C buyers, B2B purchasers really need to find out about an expected merchant through fun, intuitive encounters (regardless of whether they don't figure they do)!

Actually—paying little heed to how B2B purchasers may state they'd want to find out about an organization—energy is the thing that makes everybody's days more brilliant. Furthermore, indeed, that incorporates your B2B possibilities! We can't fail to remember that they're standard individuals changing in accordance with a pandemic, much the same as you and me.

Thus, don't rest on the B2B client experience. Gamifying it implies that possibilities and clients will be left with a good inclination about your image. Furthermore, leaving your possibilities and clients with a good inclination about your image in the midst of a worldwide pandemic? That is precious.

Gamification in B2B Marketing

54% of B2B advertisers state they get more an incentive from occasions than some other type of promoting. In any case, when in-person occasions aren't an alternative (expresses gratitude toward Corona!), what's an advertiser to do? Gamification is an incredible elective course to offering the benefit that in-person occasions are commonly known for. Like an occasion, it cultivates collaboration and significant levels of commitment.

"The primary purpose for B2B brands grasping gamification is the inconceivable open door that it makes to screen and quantify commitment with the intended interest group... B2B advertisers can use the unexpected fever for games as a component of an incorporated mission."

Besides, late exploration shows that among now and 2025 "North America is relied upon to have the most noteworthy piece of the pie" for gamification in the field of advertising", and it's "extended to observe the most noteworthy fuse of gamification frameworks in big business level arrangements".

So as opposed to giving a possibility a song and dance on why they should purchase from your B2B organization, take a stab at drawing in with your possibilities in a fun and lively manner. Gamification may very well make the deal for you! Keep B2B clients returning with these gamification thoughts:

Basic games like random data, or more perplexing games like a forager chase through geolocation-empowered application

Weave gamification/intuitiveness into messages to support reaction rates on UGC (client created content) crusade

Intuitive email components that drive commitment

Vivified catches and CTAs

Rollover impacts to feature items

Intelligent item picture merry go rounds constrained by the email beneficiary

Accordion highlights to make long-shape messages more minimized

Reviews, surveys, and UGIC (client produced intelligent substance)

As an advertiser, it's difficult to make and keep a flourishing B2B brand network. The arrangement is to gamify client confronting content. This will pull in leads while additionally holding the brand network through all the more captivating encounters.

Examples of overcoming adversity

The B2B gamification techniques recorded above are distinct advantages, yet don't take it from me—take it from associations that have executed this pattern in intelligent showcasing and never thought back:

One of the previous examples of overcoming adversity comes from 2009, when IBM's Innov8 stage "gamified the preparation cycle and turned into a moment hit inside a couple of long periods of going live… For IBM, Innov8 was the top lead generator."

"For B2B organizations, for example, Oracle, Cisco, and Salesforce, gamification has arisen as a critical component in their consumerization of the endeavor system."

"These associations are pulled in by gamification's capacity to raise commitment and dependability, estimated as expected, nearby, rehash visits, and viral circulation by a normal of 30%. Aside from commitment, gamification's income impacts are likewise great. American worldwide programming organization, Autodesk raised its preliminary use by 40% and change rates by 15% while Extraco Bank raised its client acquisitions by 700%."

How Gamification Fits into the Big Picture

B2B associations should regard gamification as a drawn out technique that goes through incessant advancements to guarantee the advertising stays applicable. Advertisers should mean to actualize gamification across various channels to connect each prospect or client in a liquid, sweeping experience.

Has your B2B image previously executed email computerization for lead age? Need to both pull in possibilities and hold clients in an interestingly captivating manner? It seems as though you're prepared to gamify your B2B promoting and CX procedure.

9

How to include Gamification as part of your Marketing Mix

Gamification is an advanced showcasing term used to portray the activity of applying run of the mill elements, structure, and strategies of game playing to non-gaming conditions, for example, business, instruction, wellbeing, and promoting among numerous others.

Gamification has a definitive objective of profoundly captivating the client. The qualities of game playing make it a lot simpler for clients to recognize themselves with the substance and brand behind the game.

Numerous brands are gradually finding that gamification can be an incredible partner with regards to advanced promoting. Advertisers can now rapidly, effectively and absent a lot of exertion accomplish their showcasing objectives and draw in their crowd.

The most widely recognized destinations that can be accomplished with the utilization of gamification are:

Expanded brand mindfulness – clients are bound to draw in with games than with some other online substance.

Pull in the clients' consideration

Increment commitment

Acquire steadfastness

Produce leads

Gain adherents

Make excellent substance

Engage

Increment traffic

Advise

Advance items and administrations

Inspire

Increment interest

marked smaller than usual games are too useful with regards to accomplishing advertising destinations.

Word Search will expand traffic to your site

To finish a Word search, you would typically give the client the words that they need to discover. In any case, if your advertising objective is to direct people to your site or blog, don't show the concealed words on a similar screen! All things considered, as a feature of your showcasing methodology, you can find an outside connection in the header of the application. It will divert the crowd to a page that you are attempting to advance, and that is the place where the shrouded words will be shown. This way you produce additional traffic to your blog or site, as without visiting the website page the game can't be finished.

When the client knows all the words they require to search for they will return to the past page and resolve the game. For our situation, the shrouded words are virality, devotees, reliability, adaptability, and straightforwardness.

To make this model we have utilized the "Shroud the legend" alternative in the Word Search board. This way the client should check the shrouded words in the substance that we allude to. The target of this model was to send traffic to a site and to illuminate the client about the items and administrations offered by the brand.

Gamification is additionally an incredible instrument to acquire information, engage the crowd and make top notch content. You can likewise present items and administrations, yet in addition stand out and increment client commitment.

Puzzle will help you focus on a specialty crowd

Suppose you're a gallery chief attempting to assemble information of future historical center guests. You make an online Puzzle and offer it via web-based media networks, requesting your adherents to arrange sequentially various works from workmanship.

In this sort of advancement, you will discover two distinct kinds of clients. There will be specialists that have the information to finish the game since they're keen on craftsmanship. In any case, there will be additionally individuals who won't have the option to complete the Puzzle without doing on the web research.

To make this model we have utilized the "Shroud the legend" alternative in the Word Search board. This way the client should check the concealed words in the substance that we allude to. The goal of this model was to send traffic to a site and to advise the client about the items and administrations offered by the brand.

Gamification is additionally an awesome instrument to get information, engage the crowd and make great substance. You can likewise present items and administrations, yet additionally stand out and increment client commitment.

Puzzle will help you focus on a specialty crowd

Suppose you're an exhibition hall chief attempting to accumulate information of future gallery guests. You make an online Puzzle and offer it via web-based media networks, requesting your adherents to arrange sequentially various works from workmanship.

In this kind of advancement, you will discover two unique sorts of clients. There will be specialists that have the information to finish the game since they're keen on workmanship. However, there will be likewise individuals who won't have the option to complete the Puzzle without doing on the web research.

Toward the finish of the game, you will have data about the members that finished the Puzzle in the briefest time. However, aside from arriving at your specialty crowd, you will likewise have educated a more extensive number regarding on the web clients about a subject that they were curious about with. This may create their advantage, making them expected future clients. As in the past model, the gaming application accomplishes something beyond one advertising objective. It illuminates, produces excellent substance and pulls in the consideration of a more extensive crowd.

Memory: Promote items and administrations

Gamification in showcasing has additionally another reason. Brands use games as an additional apparatus to publicize and advance their items and administrations, it is called advergaming, and it is the improvement of games used to advance items and administrations.

Eye to eye with the Christmas season, there are a great many organizations that are attempting to help their deals and convince people in general to pick their image more than several others. Winter occasions are the pinnacle season for shopping centers, particularly toys and aroma shops however sweets and baked goods likewise go like hotcakes!

An advertiser of an organization that encounters a major ascent in benefits during Christmas will need to advance the top rated items to a more extensive crowd, and this can be accomplished with a snappy and simple Memory game. Through a game this way, you open your crowd to the items that you need to advance, as you pick the photos that the clients will attempt to coordinate.

Before the finish of the game, the members will have been presented to the items many occasions. Thusly the brand attention to your organization will be expanded, and the crowd will have the option to separate your items from the contenders'.

10

Gamification as part of your Content Marketing Strategy

Gamification can possibly upset your substance promoting procedure – models and tips to tell the best way to apply it

Content showcasing is anticipated to keep on being a vital technique in computerized advertising and advertisers will before long beginning searching for new answers for make fun and connecting with content. Huge numbers of them are now inspired by gamification – investigator Gartner anticipates that by 2016, gamified procedures will become standard practice for driving brand commitment and encouraging customer faithfulness. Here are a couple of tips to assist you with understanding the potential gamification holds for reforming your substance advertising technique.

Gamification

The essentials

Above all else, what is gamification? It's essentially utilization of game systems to non-gaming exercises and settings. Gamification is of extraordinary use to regions of business which rely upon commitment and inspiration – for example preparing, venture the executives, enlistment or advertising.

Compensating players with focuses and identifications or showing top players on uncommon leaderboards, advertisers can interest the serious idea of people and effectively draw in purchasers with the brand.

Advantages and dangers

For what reason are advertisers intrigued by gamification by any means? The primary favorable position of gamified conditions is that they basically drive inspiration. Applying gamification to content advertising, advertisers can make numerous open doors for shopper commitment with brands, drive explicit practices and rouse players to perform errands which require a great deal of exertion or time and would be outlandish in non-gamified conditions.

Be that as it may, advertisers keen on utilizing gamified procedures for making all the more captivating substance should know about dangers engaged with gamification also. On the off chance that games are ineffectively planned or severely directed, they neglect to convey the normal outcomes and might carry genuine results to brand's standing. A few games flash discussion – recall the enlisting game dispatched by the US Army?

To ensure that their gamified practice is protected and carries substantial impacts to content showcasing, advertisers should take additional consideration when planning the game and defining rules, give input progressively, legitimately perceive top players and gain ground following straightforward.

Gamification in real life

Up until now, gamification found a ton of increase by carrying extraordinary outcomes to solid brands everywhere on the world. Here are 3 instances of outstandingly beneficial utilization of gamified systems for content advertising.

Heineken US Open Instagram challenge

During the 2013 US Open, Heineken dispatched a "Air out the US" challenge on an uncommon Instagram account. Advertisers set up more than 200 photographs to form a mosaic demonstrating a tennis match crowd. Customers needed to follow hints remembered for photograph inscriptions, arrive at the last photograph, leave a remark and dominate match tickets. It was fundamentally a ticket giveaway dependent on an unpredictable photograph chase.

The challenge endured 3 days and highlighted an aggregate of 7 occasions, carrying in excess of 1500 clients to partake in the game. Accordingly, Heineken noticed an amazing 20% expansion in devotee number on their @Heineken_US account and delighted in a ton of presentation as one of the primary US Open patrons. Despite the fact that the photograph chase was confounded, buyers felt propelled to proceed and tackle the riddle.

M&M's Eye-Spy Pretzel

M&M's took gamified content showcasing to the following level in 2013, when the brand dispatched the M&M's Pretzel crusade. The occasion was made out of a wide range of parts – among them a straightforward eye-spy game. The brand distributed a huge realistic brimming with M&M's on its Facebook account. The errand of clients was straightforward – locate the minuscule pretzel tucked away among the treats.

The game was met with extraordinary energy – it immediately became a web sensation, producing loads of commotion via web-based media. Here's the first post – you can see with your own eyes that it got more than 25,000 preferences, 6,000 offers and 11,000 remarks.

It may from the start appear to be extraordinary that clients would really need to invest energy searching for the little pretzel and afterward share the game with their companions, yet the movement unmistakably engaged every one of the individuals who played comparative games all through their youth.

Delight Hunt by Magnum Ice Cream

In the event that you felt that gamification for content advertising was a moderately novel issue, think about this: generally in 2011 Magnum utilized this system in a savvy online ability game called the Pleasure Hunt. The game's fourth version as of late went with Magnum's 25th birthday celebration. You can in any case play its first version here.

In the entirety of its versions, players would just control a character, the 'Magnum Woman', and their primary assignment was to help her gather chocolates as the character bounced starting with one site then onto the next, visiting brands going from Samsung and Dove to Saab or even YouTube. Moving around page mockups, the character immediately drew in players and the game immediately turned into a web sensation.

Magnum Pleasure Hunt was energizing in itself, yet it was likewise very much coordinated with Magnum's social channels. Finishing the joy chase, players could share their outcomes to their organizations on Facebook and Twitter and challenge their companions to beat their outcomes.

How to begin utilizing gamification in your substance showcasing system at the present time?

You don't need to be a piece of a huge association or work on a huge promoting spending plan to fuse gamified methodologies into your substance showcasing. Gamification can work for practically any item or administration and it's versatile to each financial plan. Here are a couple of tips to assist you with beginning on gamification for content promoting.

1. Make little strides

In the event that you've never attempted gamification in promoting, its best to initially attempt it with a straightforward game so you can figure out how hypothesis functions practically speaking and perceive how your intended interest group gets the game. One approach to begin is by compensating clients for visiting your Facebook page, following you on Twitter or review your recordings on YouTube.

2. Structure your game to sort out it

In the event that your prize framework is unpredictable to the point that it expects clients to get acquainted with a long manual to get it, you're never going to get agreeable outcomes from gamification. Rather than building a huge and confounded gamified climate, it's smarter to separate the game into a bunch of little exercises which guests can find out about step by step. Give players simply the data they totally need to have to move to the following level.

3. Relate gamification to your advertising objectives

Plan your gamification methodology to guarantee that guests don't simply visit your site to play and afterward leave the page. Gamification is there to assist you with making item mindfulness or increment your primary concern. Your game should guide guests to different pieces of your site, studying your item or administration.

4. Talk with experts

Gamification can be precarious and gravely planned showcasing games happen more frequently than you'd anticipate. In the event that you as of now have a couple of duties on your back and adding one will be excessively, you can in any case make the most from gamified conditions by utilizing items and administrations of organizations, for example, Badgeville or Gigya which have practical experience in making gamification programs.

Gamification is an astounding methodology to help you zest up your substance advertising and connect with your intended interest group in new manners by giving an extraordinary client experience, encouraging purchaser steadfastness and building a positive picture of your image.

11

How to make your marketing go Viral?

Viral substance is any bit of media that turns out to be fiercely mainstream short-term.

It very well may be a Youtube video, Facebook post, tweet, or practically any online media content that gets shared a great many occasions.

Viral substance begins to work for you on autopilot, as your image gets presented to an entirely different crowd that you couldn't actually very reach naturally.

You may think getting your substance to become famous online is as likely as you hitting the lottery, however nothing could be further from reality. In case you're hoping to create buzz for your business or on the off chance that you simply need your own 15 minutes of notoriety, keep perusing.

Tip: Jeff utilizes SEMrush to investigate SEO-improved substance thoughts, make high-performing substance, and screen its presentation.

Here are some fast however sure approaches to accomplish the equivalent:

1. Plan for web crawler control

Doubtlessly, web indexes convey the most supportable and long haul traffic to sites. In this way, to make your substance advertising become famous online, recognize conceivably popular and low-rivalry watchword expressions and afterward improve your substance for these words.

Need an approach to improve this cycle? SEMrush's Keyword Tool is the ideal arrangement. This apparatus;

Uncovers more than 2 million watchword thoughts.

Empowers you to fragment catchphrases into gatherings.

Picks the best watchwords dependent on whether you can rank for them.

Evaluate SEMrush for nothing here.

2. Individuals need to look keen (so let them)

At the point when individuals consider sharing substance, they think about social money. In the event that it makes them look shrewd or savvy, the almost certain they are to pass it onto their companions and adherents.

In February of 2012, LinkedIn conveyed messages to choose individuals that were essential for the main 5 percent of most saw profiles for the earlier year.

A large number of individuals ran to Facebook and Twitter to get out the great word. The greatest recipient of this was LinkedIn on the grounds that it raised its profile and likely got a large number of new individuals.

3. Keep it short

By far most of viral substance is short. Recordings will in general go from around 30 seconds to one moment. Anything longer and you may lose your hold.

Tip: Use devices, for example, InVideo to make dazzling proficient level recordings in minutes with pre-made layouts.

The equivalent goes for online journals. Individuals have short considerations ranges; so make it simple for them with "searchable" substance, for example, pictures, spot focuses and subheadings.

4. Take a human point

Transformers to make your substance advertising circulate around the web

Maybe you have discovered the ideal beverage to have on your wedding commemoration? Possibly you need to share a few characteristics your supervisor has that you scorn, and you figure the vast majority can identify with?

In the event that individuals can relate and apply it to their own lives, they are significantly more prone to share. When something is close to home to somebody, they will pass it on.

5. Make it certified

A great many people are not searching for recordings or web journals that appear to be profoundly delivered or exaggerated. There should be a certified vibe.

A "how to" manage is a genuine model, and recordings in the background of a fascinating occasion is additionally a phenomenal model.

6. Go intelligent

Do you have master information on an intriguing subject?

Individuals need and expect content they can talk about, and the more this is valid, the more it your substance will get shared.

Intelligent substance, for example, tests are an incredible method to do this.

7. Allow perusers to remark

Perusers remarking to make your substance advertising circulate around the web

On the off chance that you are a blogger, you need a decent remark segment framework, for example, Disqus, in the event that you need an opportunity to become a web sensation.

In the event that you get a decent remark or a dubious one, react to it. A decent network of individuals remarking will consistently build your opportunity of virality.

8. Use records and pictures

Records and pictures on Twitter to make your substance showcasing circulate around the web

Individuals love records and pictures.

In the event that you make your blog entry a rundown, your odds of turning into a web sensation increment an incredible arrangement. On the off chance that you, at that point cushion out that rundown with some imaginative symbolism, you increment your viral possibilities considerably more.

9. Make a convincing feature

Convincing feature model for make your substance advertising circulate around the web

With such a huge amount of substance out there today, you should establish an incredible first connection, or you'll be passed for another.

Make your feature snappy, advantage driven and inquisitive…

A decent analysis, is to inquire;

"Would I click on that feature?"

10. Try not to cause anybody to feel stupid

Large mustache and cigarette to make your substance showcasing circulate around the web

Picture Source: Pixabay

At the point when individuals share content, they are really risking their own standing for all to see. So be mindful so as not to distance gatherings or down talk minorities.

Well known people, then again, are regularly reasonable game. For instance, the official run of Donald Trump is a questionable subject. On the off chance that you uphold him or not, there is sufficient data out there to help either view, and you make certain to get a response from those on the two sides of the fence.

11. Make posts proper

Facebook posts for make your substance promoting become famous online

In the event that you will post on Facebook, ensure you utilize appropriate sentence structure and designing to make your substance intelligible. Nothing is more irritating than one major, enormous, long passage.

On the off chance that you will Tweet, don't utilize each of the 140 characters. Make certain to leave at any rate 10 to 12 spaces (this aides for empowering re-tweets).

Getting your substance advertising to circulate around the web is certifiably not a definite science using any and all means. However, on the off chance that you follow these demonstrated rules, you can surely build your opportunity of having a viral blog, Tweet or offer that gets you the introduction you need.